D1267217

GIFT OF

John Warren Stewig

Carthage

MUD, MOON AND ME

MUD, MOON AND ME

Poems by
ZARO WEIL

Illustrations by
JO BURROUGHES

Houghton Mifflin Company
Boston   1992

Library of Congress Cataloging-in-Publication Data

Weil, Zaro.
   Mud, moon, and me : poems / by Zaro Weil ; illustrations by Jo
Burroughes.—1st American ed.
       p.   cm.
   "Originally published in Great Britain in 1989 by Orchard Books"—
T. p. verso.
   Summary: An illustrated collection of poems on a variety of
topics.
   ISBN 0-395-58038-2
   1. Children's poetry, English.   [1. English poetry.]
I. Burroughes, Joanna, ill.   II. Title.
PR6045.E45M8   1992   91-19922
821'.914—dc20   CIP
                             AC

Printed in the United States of America

BP 10 9 8 7 6 5 4 3 2 1

For my children Victoria and Gideon

Zaro Weil

CONTENTS

Wake Up   11

The Sun Queen
Morning   13

How to Get an Idea   14

Tiny Moon   15

It's Monday   16

The Paper Bag   18

A Boy and His Dog   21

When I was the Sunrise   22

When I was the Sunset   23

A Walk   25

Two Pussycats   26

The Car Ride   29

From My Window   31

Have a Good Laugh   32

Mud   34

When I was the Grass   36

When I was the Wind   37

Our Dog   38

The Weed   41

Questions and Answers   42

The Sun Queen
    Afternoon   45

Horse   46

Winter   47

Waiting   49

If It Were My Birthday   50

A Trade   52

Cherry Blossoms   53

The Hare and the Pheasant
    and the Sparrow   54

When I was the Sky   56

When I was the Forest   58

My Eyes   60

Unicorn   61

An October Wind   62

The Ladybird   65

Shadows   67

My Dog   69

When I was a Mouse   70

When I was a Dragon   71

Ten-Minute Poem   72

Me and the Earthworm   73

The Sun Queen
    Evening   75

It's Easy to Dream   76

Fireflies   79

Night Sky   80

WAKE UP

Wake up

Morning
Has
Galloped
Bareback
All night to
Get here

THE SUN QUEEN
Morning

She: Rise sun.

Sun: Yes your majesty.

She: Shine sun.

Sun: Yes your majesty.

She: Warm me.

Sun: A pleasure.

She: And sun.

Sun: Yes?

She: Make this a zoo day.

How to Get an Idea

Dig into mud
>   or
Open up a new box of crayons
>   or
Run your fingers through a bag of marbles
>   or
Skip a stone across water
>   or
Ask a cat to lend you one
>   or
Stand quietly under a dictionary
>   or
Stick out your tongue and say, "Ah!"
>   or
Put an empty picture frame on the wall and wait

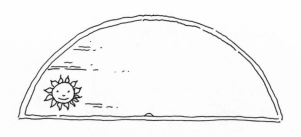

TINY MOON

Tiny moon

Even a
Penny
Could eclipse you
This morning

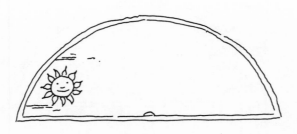

It's Monday

It's Monday   my sore hurts
It's Tuesday   my hair is growing
It's Wednesday   my hands are clean
It's Thursday   my muscle is big
It's Friday   my tongue touches my nose
It's Saturday   my legs turn cartwheels
It's Sunday   my arm has a freckle
It's Monday   I'm still me
             only more

THE PAPER BAG

Fill up a paper bag with
Spring sounds and
Open it in December

Fill up a paper bag with
Snow flurries and
Use them to decorate your bedroom

Fill up a paper bag with
Ribbons and
Fly them when you want a word with the wind

Fill up a paper bag with
Winter quiet and
Open it when it's time to be alone

Fill up a paper bag with
Your favourite words and
Shake it till a good story comes out

Fill up a paper bag with
Secrets and
Share them with a friend every so often

Fill up a paper bag with
Velvet
Just to have it

A Boy and His Dog

Boy: Here dog
Dog: Woof
Boy: Good dog
Dog: Woof woof
Boy: Now sit
Dog: Woof woof woof
Boy: Now stand
Dog: Woof woof woof woof
Boy: Roll over
Dog: Woof woof woof woof woof
Boy: Now speak
Dog: Here boy

When I was the Sunrise

When I was
the
sunrise
sunset
used
to
wait
for
me
every
day

WHEN I WAS THE SUNSET

When I was
the
sunset
sunrise
used
to
wait
for
me
every
night

A WALK

Count the spots
And the lines the crooked
Designs the lacing of here to there
The colours of threads
In directions of webs
Paper scraps
Bumps and cracks
That form into rows
Of curves that go
Into puzzles
I solve
Very slowly

Two Pussycats

Two pussycats
Playing
Pawed in my
Snowgarden
Arching
Circling
Rolling like it were
Summer and
Goldenrod had
Flown in their noses

THE CAR RIDE

Boy: Why are you racing, trees?

Trees: Because you are-r-r-r-r.

Boy: But look. I'm sitting still!

Trees: That's what you think-k-k-k-k-k.

Boy: Well, the last one to the traffic light
is a monkey's uncle!

Trees: You're on-n-n-n-n-n.

FROM MY WINDOW

The waters fall in rectangles
Cities sprout umbrellas
Clear water paints a blurred picture
Tears slide from afternoon branches
Dirt breathes a deep sigh of mud
It's raining today

HAVE A GOOD LAUGH

Have a good laugh

There is so much rain today
The whole earth came
To take a look
And
Stayed on

Now have another laugh

There is so much sun today
The whole earth came
To take a look
And
Went off in a spin

MUD

It squelches and belches
A spattering flop
A morass of dense goop
That gurges in glops

Now seeping now weeping
A popple a spurt
A lagoon of brown pudding
Some very wet dirt

It burbles so blustery
And spills out its custardy
Bubbles that pop
From bottom to top

To squeeze between toes
And squish as it goes
All oozy and flabby
Dank deep and slabby

Oh
No
So
Slow

What a lazy muddle
What a hiccup of a puddle

WHEN I WAS THE GRASS

When I was
the grass
I bowed
to the wind

now that
I'm the mountain-top
no one can
tell me anything

WHEN I WAS THE WIND

When I was the wind
I travelled
all the time

now that
I'm a rock
I have a lot
of time
inside of me

Our Dog

Our dog barked all the time
Each day he barked
Forgetting how he barked
The day before

The first year he barked
With spring mud under his chin
And then in summer
When the mud had dried
He barked at the green snake
Of a garden hose
He barked through the flying
Of the autumn sycamore leaves
And barked circles
In the lighthearted snow

He barked at neighbourhood dogs, cats
Squirrels, birds of any colour
At the children playing tag
At the snails, soft bugs, flies
Lawnmower hums
Anything

Then when spring came again
And the moist April earth
Caked to the fringes of his fur
He died

Maybe it was too much for him
Barking at the violets as they grew

THE WEED

Boy: Father. Come quick!
Father: What is it, boy? Is anything wrong? What happened?
Boy: I did it!
Father: Did what?
Boy: I pulled this weed out of the ground.
Father: That's good. You're very strong today.
Boy: You bet I'm strong. I was pulling one way, and the whole earth was pulling the other way, and I won!

QUESTIONS AND ANSWERS

Q: What's inside the sun?

A: Daytime.

Q: What's inside the earth?

A: Colours before they get their names.

Q: Who made the first circle?

A: Someone who got very dizzy.

Q: What draws the bee to the honeysuckle?

A: Ten million summers.

Q: What roars inside a seashell?

A: Beach lions.

Q: What roars inside of you?

A: My blood.

Q: How does one tie a rainbow?

A: The first thing is to find the ends.

Q: If it's noon here, what time is it on Mars?

A: A billion years before noon.

Q: How long does it take to move a mountain?

A: Depends on the number of ants available.

Q: At what speed does a moth move to a lamp?

A: At light speed.

Q: Why is the letter 'i' dotted?

A: To have a good time.

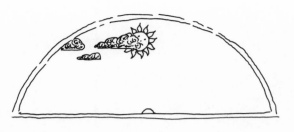

THE SUN QUEEN
Afternoon

She: Sun.

Sun: My queen.

She: Where have you gone?

Sun: Behind the cloud.

She: Won't you come out?

Sun: I'm afraid I can't.

She: Is there nothing to do?

Sun: You could call the wind.

She: Good. Where is the wind?

Sun: Behind the rain.

She: Where is the rain?

Sun: Hidden in a cloud.

She: Which one?

Sun: I don't know. I can't see from
here.

She: You play too many games.

HORSE

What is it you hear horse
When you arch your head
To the ground
Is there a story
Of brown
Of green
In the sweet clotted earth you inhale
In the feather grass that brushes your cheek

What is it you see horse
When you run along that crack
Of land
Of sky
Tell me
For I too long to part the wind
With my head
For I too ache for a story

Winter

Winter
Hold your breath
This air is
Mud fresh
And runs thick
With spring
And deep
With the scent
Of lilac

Winter
If you only
Knew what
Lay ahead
You'd never have
Opened your mouth
At all this year

WAITING

Sometimes
I wait too long
For the next thing
To happen
And
When that
Happens I'm
Waiting for the
Next thing to
Happen

Now I
Could either

A. Keep waiting for the next thing to happen
   or
B. Keep happening and not wait at all

If It Were My Birthday

If it were my birthday
I'd be the bounce of a basketball
Or the stretch of a telephone call
I'd wrap up in a waterfall

I'd jump in and out
Of somersaults
And fall into a spin
And spin another grin

If it were my birthday
I'd be the shine of a hummingbird's flight
Or the shimmy of a wild horse fight
I'd be the silk of a bonfire light

This makes me laugh
Dandelion puffs
This makes me think
In zigzags

A Trade

I'll trade you my kingdom for your song

I'll trade you my song for your colour

I'll trade you my colour for your story

I'll trade you my story for your dance

I'll trade you my dance for your daydream

I'll trade you my daydream for your hand

I'll trade you my hand for your hand

CHERRY BLOSSOMS

Cherry blossoms
Are quiet
Unlike frogs
Leaping to every
Raindrop

THE HARE AND THE PHEASANT
AND THE SPARROW

The hare jumps
Across the
White frost field
So smooth
So sure
A summer river

A rust and polished
Pheasant
Swoops low
Through mist
With shrills
To clear his path

Sparrow
Sits on the stone wall
Does he know
Thousands have come
Before him

WHEN I WAS THE SKY

When I was
the
sky
I
collected
airplanes
balloons
mosquitoes
rockets
birds
kites
planets
meteors
clouds
flies
and
dust

now that
I'm
the
earth
I
wonder
how
I
got
so
much
air

WHEN I WAS THE FOREST

W hen I was
the
forest
it took me
one hundred years
to have a thought

now that
I'm the sea
I can change
my mind
in a second

My Eyes

My eyes
Rush to the stream

While
My feet take me to
The rest of the day

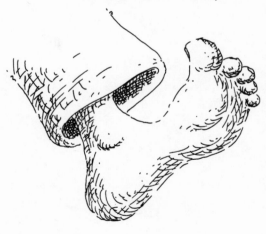

Unicorn

Unicorn
Don't go
Let me ask you how long you've been here

Please
No lies

An October Wind

An October wind
Ruffles the heavy shade of
The summer maple

Its leaves grow
Lightheaded and
Drop off in a million
Crimson circles

The tree is an
Outline of itself
Good for
Unruffling the wind

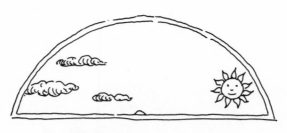

THE LADYBIRD

Remember me?
I'm the
Ladybird that
Tiptoed
Down
Your
Thumb
The afternoon
That you
Turned one.

What?
No?

I
Guess you
Were asleep.

Shadows

Moon
Last evening you
Rolled so loud and silver
Past my window
That the shadows
Woke and wove their dark
Molasses stripes
Over my bed

And
In the criss-cross of
That night-time
I knew what to do
Breathe soft
Breathe soft
And fold into a quiet silhouette
Until morning

My Dog

When
My dog
Sleeps by the fire
Not even a
Tangerine fox
Can rouse her

When I was a Mouse

When I was

a

mouse

darkness

circled

above

my

head

like

a

hawk

When I was a Dragon

When I was
a
dragon
I
spit
roaring
firewords

and
in
the
smoke
I
could
see
no
one

Ten-Minute Poem

There are only ten minutes left to go
Should I get up and get ready to leave now
Or should I keep doing this for nine minutes
     more
Or climb a tree in eight minutes
Or bake a cake in seven minutes
Or write a book in six minutes
Or make an important scientific discovery
     during the next five minutes
Or compose a symphony in four minutes
Or save my country in three minutes
Or circumnavigate the globe in two minutes
Or explore the milky way in one minute
Or or or or . . . .

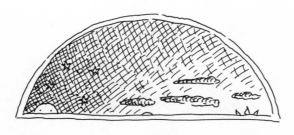

ME AND THE EARTHWORM

Me: Where are you going, Earthworm?
Earthworm: Around the world.
Me: How long will it take?
Earthworm: A long stretch.

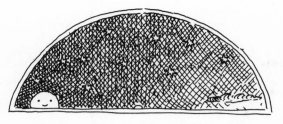

THE SUN QUEEN
Evening

She: And sun.

Sun: My queen.

She: You may not leave.

Sun: Why is that?

She: Night-time grows shadows.

Sun: But night-time grows stars.

She: All right. Goodnight sun.
And moon.

Moon: Yes?

She: No tricks tonight.

Moon: Good night your majesty.

It's Easy to Dream

It's easy to dream
Just wait for
Evening
To powder the sky
With a million thoughts

And then
Select a few for yourself

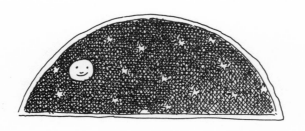

FIREFLIES

If
You collect
Enough fireflies
You could
Read secrets
Under your blanket
All night long

NIGHT SKY

Night sky
Floods my room
Oh
My heart pounds
The moon is
Now my own